A Day With

A Day With

INFLUENTIAL AMERICAN PERSONALITIES

MOONSTONE

Published in Moonstone
by Rupa Publications India Pvt. Ltd 2023
7/16, Ansari Road, Daryaganj
New Delhi 110002

Sales centres:
Prayagraj Bengaluru Chennai
Hyderabad Jaipur Kathmandu
Kolkata Mumbai

P-ISBN: 978-93-5520-932-0
E-ISBN: 978-93-5520-933-7

First impression 2023

10 9 8 7 6 5 4 3 2 1

Printed in India

Contents

Neil Armstrong

Barack Obama

John F. Kennedy

Abraham Lincoln

Neil Armstrong

Neil Armstrong was the first human to step on the Moon.
How did he become an astronaut?
What did he do after he became an astronaut?
Read on to find the answers.

Meet Frank and Fiona

Hi, I'm Frank.

Hi, I'm Fiona. We are going to visit Neil Armstrong. Let's meet him now.

Neil Armstrong was born in Wapakoneta, **United States of America** on 5 August, 1930.
He was a test **pilot** and an **astronaut**.

As a young boy, Neil Armstrong fell in love with airplanes.

So, he worked at an airport and took flying lessons.
He got his pilot's license when he was only 16 years old.
He could then fly airplanes.

Neil Armstrong joined the U.S. Navy as a pilot.
He trained to fly jet airplanes in **Florida.**
He **was** the young**est** pilot in **his** group.
He was sent to **Korea** and fought in many air battles.
He won three medals for his bravery.

Neil Armstrong went to **NASA** and trained to be an astronaut.
He had to learn many things. The training was long and hard.
He trained for four years.

Armstrong learned about working in a spacecraft.
He learned about the Moon. The Moon has little **gravity**,
which is the force that holds people and things to the ground.
Due to **less gravity**, **things** float on the Moon.
He learned how to do experiments while floating.

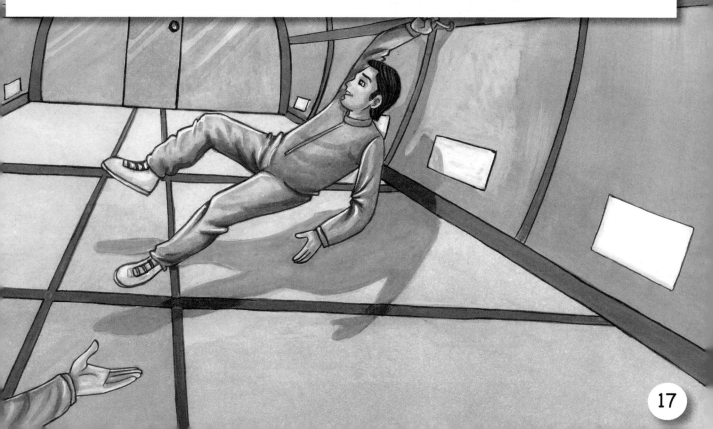

In 1966, Neil Armstrong flew into **space**. This was **his first** flight into space. He rode in the spacecraft Gemini 8. He was in **space** for 10 hours.

Armstrong did many experiments in space. He faced many problems. Once, he had to make an emergency landing in the **Pacific Ocean**. But he learned a lot about space travel through these experiences.

In 1969, Neil Armstrong flew into space again.
He was the commander of the first mission to the Moon.
The mission was called "Apollo 11".
Two other astronauts were also part of the mission. They were Michael Collins and Edwin E. Aldrin, Jr.

They flew on a space shuttle called the Columbia, which took four days to reach the Moon.

Chapter 7: First Man on the Moon

On 20 July, 1969, Neil Armstrong became the first human to land on the Moon.
It was a great day for everyone!

Armstrong said the famous words, "One small step for man, one giant leap for mankind."

Neil Armstrong travelled around the world.
He shared his experiences of landing on
the Moon with millions of people.
He became very famous.

In 1971, Armstrong left NASA.
He **decided to do something** new.
He became a professor at the **University of Cincinnati**, where he taught about space and spacecraft.

Neil Armstrong was the first human to walk on the Moon.
An air and space **museum** is named after him.
It is in **Ohio** in the United States of America.

He died in Cincinnati, USA on 25 August, 2012.

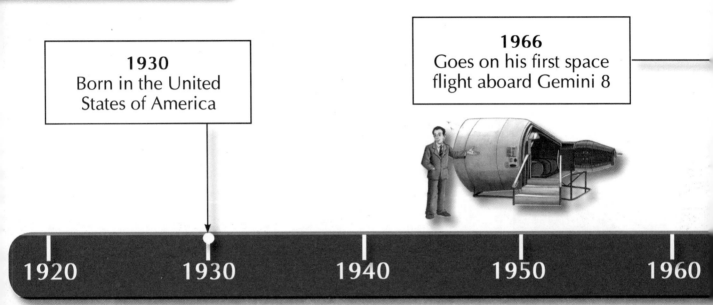

1930
Born in the United
States of America

1966
Goes on his first space
flight aboard Gemini 8

1920   1930   1940   1950   1960

1962
Becomes a test pilot and
flies many fighter jets

Neil Armstrong's Life and Work

1969
Becomes the first person
to step on the Moon

1970   1980   1990   2000   2020

1971
Leaves NASA. He
becomes a professor
at the University of
Cincinnati

2012
Dies in the United
States of America

Word Meanings

Astronaut: A person who is trained to travel in spacecrafts

Florida: A state in the southeastern part of the United States of America

Gravity: The force that causes objects to have weight

Honour: A sign of special respect or admiration

Korea: A country in northeast Asia

Museum: A place where people can see valuable objects

NASA: National Aeronautics and Space Administration, a space agency in the United States of America

Ohio: A state in the northeastern part of the United States of America

Pacific Ocean: The largest ocean in the world

Pilot: A person who is professionally trained to fly an airplane

United States: A large country in North America

University of Cincinnati: A university in Ohio, United States of America

Think, Talk and Write

Think About It

Neil Armstrong did many things before he became an astronaut.
What did you find the most interesting? Why?
Write one or two sentences to explain your answer.

Talk About It

How would you describe Armstrong?
Tell your friends about him.
Tell your friends what was Armstrong's greatest accomplishment.

Write About It

Would you like to be an astronaut?
Write about why you would or would not like to be an astronaut.

What did you learn from Neil Armstrong?

....

....

....

....

....

....

....

....

....

....

....

....

....

....

What are the five things that you
will change after reading
Neil Armstrong's story?

....
....
....
....
....
....
....
....
....
....
....
....
....
....
....

Barack Obama

Barack Obama was the forty-fourth President of the United States of America.

He was a great political leader. He was the first African–American President of the United States of America.

Meet Jeff and Jenny

Chapter 1: At the White House

Barack H. Obama was born on 4 August, 1961 in Honolulu, USA.
He became the **President** of the United States of America on 20 January, 2009 and served till 20 January, 2017.

Barack Obama's father was Barack Hussain Obama Sr.
He lived in Kenya, Africa. There, he worked for the
government of Kenya.
His mother was Stanley Ann Dunham. She was from Kansas,
United States of America. She was an **anthropologist.**
Obama's parents separated when he was just two years old
and later, they got divorced.

Chapter 3: Off to Indonesia

Barack Obama's mother remarried in 1965. His stepfather, Lolo Soetoro, was an Indonesian national.

Young Obama moved to Jakarta, Indonesia, with his family in 1967.

While in Indonesia, his sister Maya was born. Young Obama attended school until fourth grade in Indonesia.

Chapter 4: Life with Grandparents

Did you like living with your grandparents?

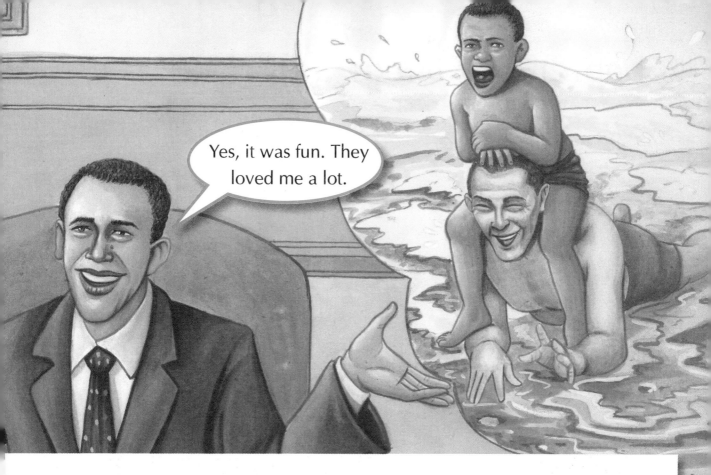

When Barack Obama was 10, his mother sent him back to Honolulu to live with his grandparents.

He continued school in Hawaii. He was a good student.

At school, his favourite subject was Mathematics.

One day, while in school, the teacher asked the class to write an essay on "My Dream: What I Want to Be".

Obama wrote, "I want to be the President."

After school, Barack Obama joined Occidental College, Los Angeles in 1979.

He studied law for two years and moved to Columbia College, New York. There he studied political science.

He graduated in 1983.

After college, he worked as a **community organizer** in **Harlem**. He also worked for a **social services organization** in Chicago. There he worked for the rights of poor people. In 1988, Obama joined Harvard Law School. He graduated from Harvard in 1991. He worked as a **professor** at the University of Chicago Law School from 1992 to 2004.

Michelle Obama was born on 17 January, 1964 in Chicago, United States of America. She completed her high school in 1981 from Whitney Young High School, Chicago. After this, she graduated from Princeton University. After Princeton, she joined Harvard Law School where she studied law. Michelle and Barack got married in October 1992. They have two daughters, Malia and Sasha.

Hello, children, we are happy to have you here.

Hello, Michelle.

Barack Obama began his career in **politics** when he was elected as the **senator** of Illinois in November 1996. He served as the senator of the state of Illinois from 1997 to 2004.

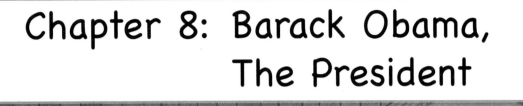

Chapter 8: Barack Obama, The President

Barack Obama was a very hard working senator.
The people of America loved him.
In February 2007, he decided to run for the presidency
of the United States of America.
In August 2008, he was declared a **nominee** of the
Democratic Party for the presidential **elections**. In
November 2008, he was elected the President of the
United States of America and served till January 2017.

Chapter 9: Conclusion

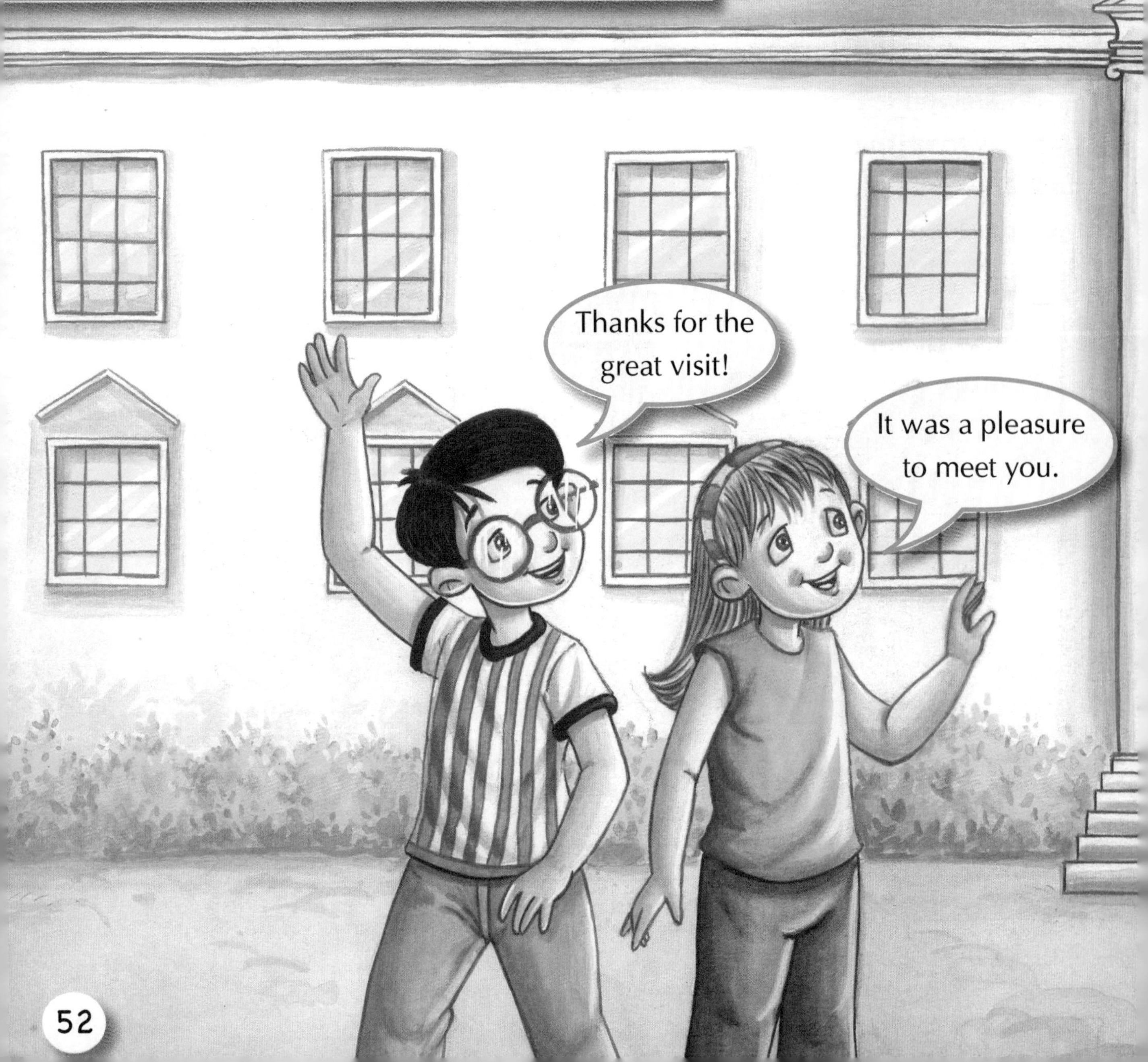

Barack Obama once remarked that his extended family is like a mini United Nations.
Just like John F. Kennedy did, Barack Obama too works towards the **equality** of black and white Americans.

1971
Returns to Hawaii to live with his maternal grandparents

1961
Born in the United States of America

1967
Moves to Jakarta to live with his family

| 1960 | 1965 | 1970 | 1975 | 1980 | 198 |

1963
His parents get separated

1979
Moves to Los Angeles to attend college

Barack H. Obama's Life and Work

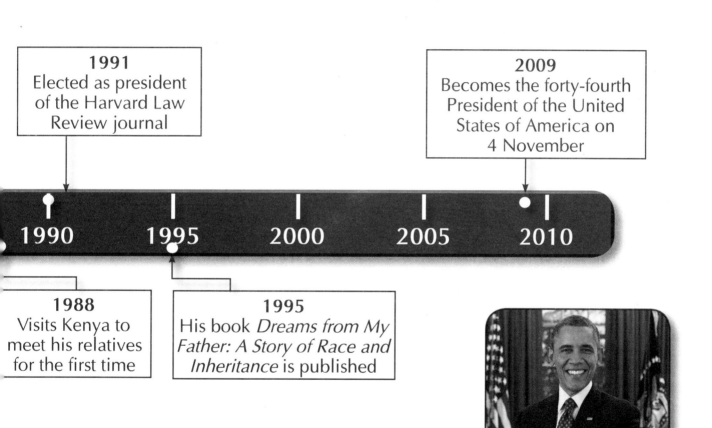

1991
Elected as president of the Harvard Law Review journal

2009
Becomes the forty-fourth President of the United States of America on 4 November

1990   1995   2000   2005   2010

1988
Visits Kenya to meet his relatives for the first time

1995
His book *Dreams from My Father: A Story of Race and Inheritance* is published

Word Meanings

President (of the USA): The head of the government

Anthropologist: A person who studies about humanity and human race

Community organizer: A person who works for people living in a community and fighting for their rights and equality

Social services organization: An organization working for the rights and benefits of people

Harlem: A place in the neighborhood of New York

Professor: A teacher in a university

Politics: The work and ideas that are connected with governing a geographical space

Senator: A member of the senate or session of parliament

Nominee: A person entitled to be awarded with something

Election: A process of voting in which public selects an individual for a post in the government office

Democratic party: One of the two political parties in the United States of America, formed in 1828

Equality: To give equal rights to all people irrespective of their caste, color, gender, orientation, etc.

Think, Talk and Write

Think About It

Glance through the chapter again and think what you felt after reading about Barack Obama's story.

Recall and count how many incidences you can remember from Obama's life.

Which part of his life attracted you the most?

Talk About It

Collect different pictures of Barack Obama and discuss about them with your friends.

Are you fascinated by Obama's life? Hold a discussion and give reasons.

What would you do if you get a chance to meet Obama?

Write About It

Try to describe Obama in your own words.

Gather more information about Michelle Obama, Malia and Sasha.

What do you want to become when you grow up? Write a few words about it.

What did you learn from Barack Obama?

....

....

....

....

....

....

....

....

....

....

....

....

....

What are the five things that you will change after reading Barack Obama's story?

....

....

....

....

....

....

....

....

....

....

....

....

....

....

John F. Kennedy

John F. Kennedy was the thirty-fifth President of the United States of America.

He was a great political leader.

As a president, Kennedy was very popular with Americans.

Meet Jeff and Jenny

Hi! I am Jeff.

Hi, I am Jenny. We are going to travel back in time to meet the great ex-president, John F. Kennedy.

John Fitzgerald Kennedy was born on 29 May, 1917 in Massachusetts, USA.

He became the President of the United States of America on 20 January, 1961 for two years.

He belonged to a wealthy and influential family.

Well, I had eight brothers and sisters.

John F. Kennedy was the second son of Joseph Patrick Kennedy. His father was a powerful businessman. John's mother, Rose Fitzgerald Kennedy, was the daughter of the mayor of Boston.
Joseph, Robert and Ted were his brothers.
Rosemary, Kathleen, Patricia, Eunice and Jean were his sisters.

John F. Kennedy went to private schools in **Connecticut**. For graduation, he opted for Harvard University. John finished college in 1940 and in the same year, published a book, titled *Why England Slept?* The book became a **bestseller** in the United States of America. It made him very popular.

It is fascinating to know you played football.

John F. Kennedy was never very healthy. He had suffered from **jaundice**, **appendicitis** and fevers in childhood. But in spite of his illness, he won a sailing championship with his brother Joseph at Harvard. John, however, never let his health issues **hamper** his dreams and **ambitions**.

My country was at war and I wanted to help it in chasing away the enemies.

John F. Kennedy joined the U.S. Navy as an intelligence officer after completing his graduation in 1941. World War II was going on and John wanted to be a part of the **combat force**. He received training in power torpedo boats.

In 1943, a Japanese ship attacked his ship. He had to save himself and his crew members.

He was awarded the Purple Heart and bravery medals for his heroic act.

John F. Kennedy left the U.S. Navy in 1945 and worked as a journalist for a short while.

After that, he worked as a member in the US House of Representatives for six years before being elected as a senator in January 1953.

In the meantime, John met Jacqueline Bouvier and got married the same year.

He worked as a **senator** for eight years before deciding to contest for the presidential poll in 1960.

John F. Kennedy won the presidential
election because of his popularity.
His family members supported him as
he became the youngest President of the
United States of America.
His most famous words from the
inaugural speech were, "Ask not what
your country can do for you; ask what
you can do for your country."

Chapter 8: Kennedy's Achievements

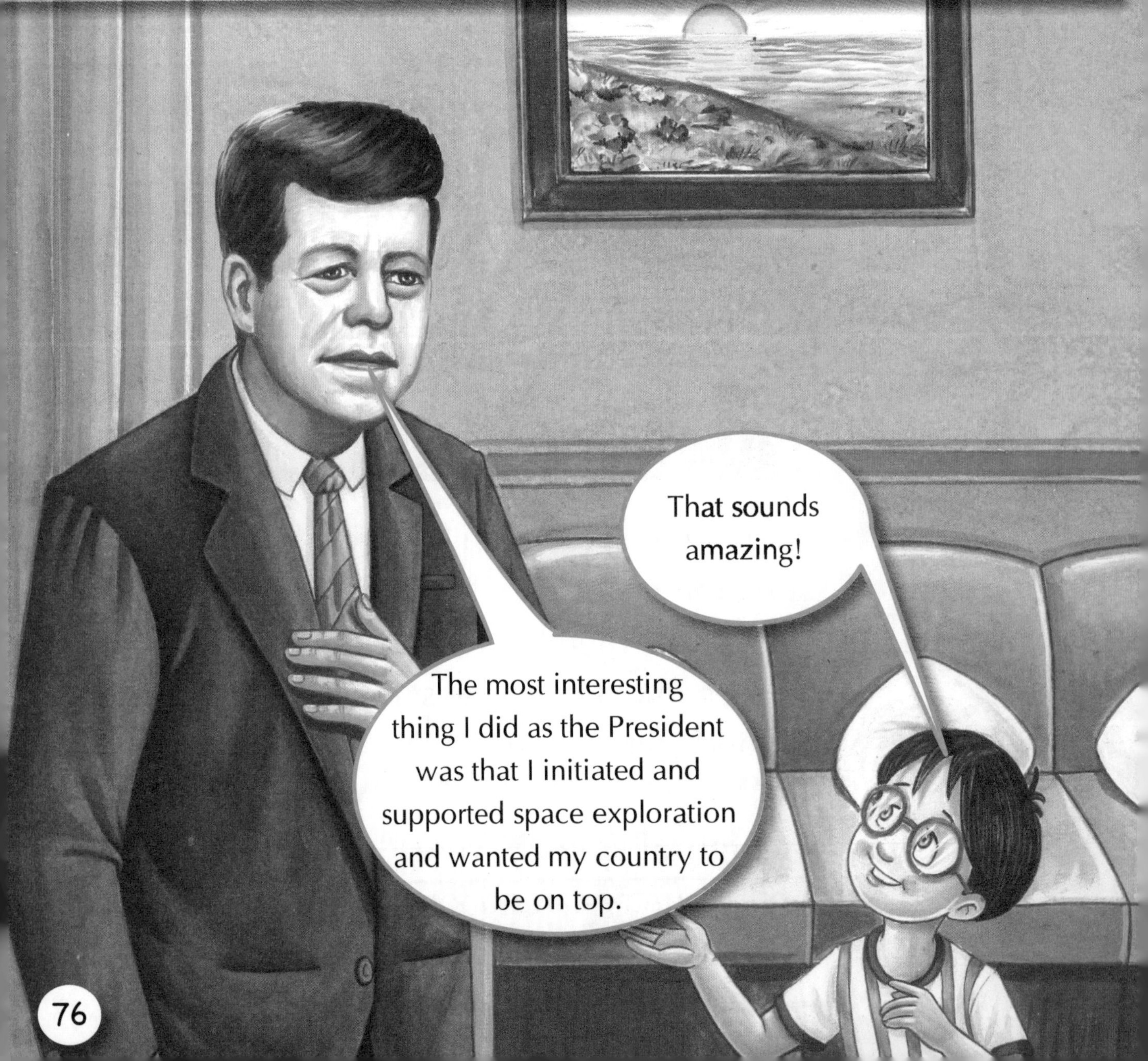

John F. Kennedy worked passionately towards the civil rights of African–Americans.

During his presidency, he worked as a **peacemaker**. He created the Peace Corps, a group that works to help people in poor nations.

Under this programme, American **volunteers** can help other nations in maintaining peace, education, healthcare and farming.

S-IV

U
N
I
T

Chapter 9: Conclusion

John F. Kennedy **motivated** people to work for their country. He was assassinated on 22 November, 1963 in Dallas, USA when he was just 46 years old. The United States of America lost its most valuable gem. His death was a great loss, as he had become an inspiration for many people. He still holds a special place in the hearts of many Americans.

1944
Wins Purple Heart and other bravery medals for saving his crew members' lives

1917
Born in the USA

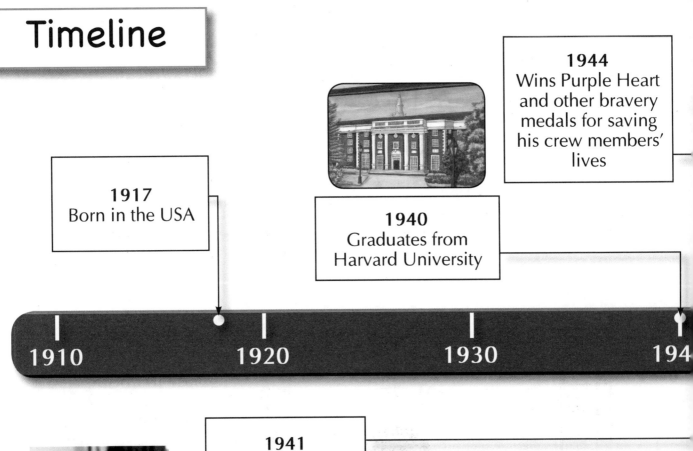

1940
Graduates from Harvard University

1910   1920   1930   194

1941
Joins the U.S. Navy

1945
Becomes a journalist

John F. Kennedy's Life and Work

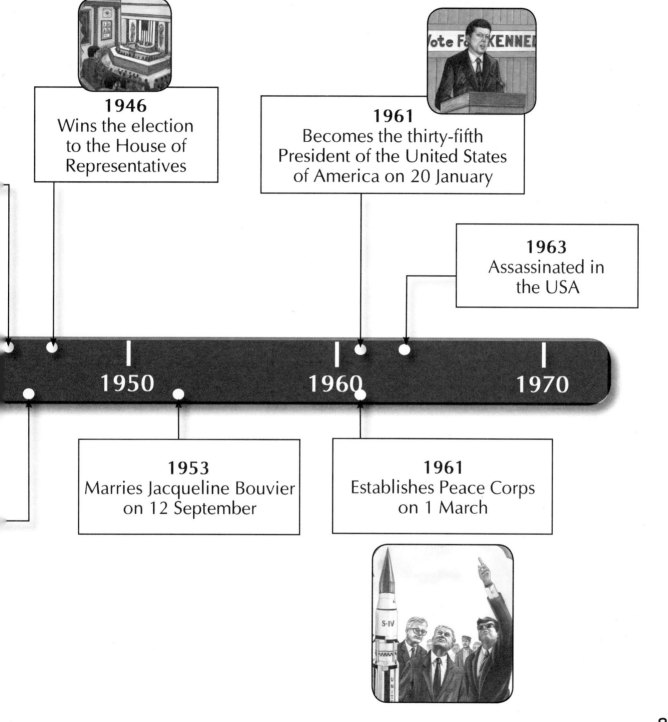

1946
Wins the election to the House of Representatives

1961
Becomes the thirty-fifth President of the United States of America on 20 January

1963
Assassinated in the USA

1950

1960

1970

1953
Marries Jacqueline Bouvier on 12 September

1961
Establishes Peace Corps on 1 March

Word Meanings

Assassinated: To murder a famous or important person, especially for political reasons

Connecticut: A state in the northeastern part of the United States of America

Bestseller: A book that has sold many copies and is in demand

Jaundice: An illness that affects the liver, and your skin and eyes turn yellow

Appendicitis: A disease of the appendix that is a long tube joined to the large intestine

Hamper: To obstruct or prevent from happening

Ambition: Something that you really want to achieve in spite of difficulties

Combat force: A battle force

Senator: A member of the senate or session of parliament

Inaugural speech: A speech made by a person to celebrate the beginning of a new job

Peacemaker: A person who is against war and favours peace

Volunteer: A person who works for social service and not for money

Motivate: To encourage one to do something

Think, Talk and Write

Think About It

Think about the reasons why people loved John F. Kennedy.
Think about the reasons why he was called people's president?

Talk About It

Recollect all the incidents from Kennedy's life.
Research about the various space programmes that Kennedy initiated and discuss it among your friends.
Have a discussion about Kennedy's life in the U.S. Navy.

Write About It

Kennedy suffered from many health problems. But, he overcame his shortcomings. Do you know any person who has done the same? If yes, then write about it.
Write about the 1943 attack on Kennedy's ship during the World War II.

What did you learn from John F. Kennedy?

....
....
....
....
....
....
....
....
....
....
....
....
....
....

What are the five things that you will change after reading John F. Kennedy's story?

....

....

....

....

....

....

....

....

....

....

....

....

....

....

Abraham Lincoln

Abraham Lincoln was a great leader.

He was one of the greatest American presidents.

He won the **American Civil War** and ended slavery in the United States of America.

Read on to learn about his life and work.

Meet Frank and Fiona

Hi, I'm Frank.

Hi, I'm Fiona.
We are going to visit
Abraham Lincoln.
Let's meet him now.

Abraham Lincoln was born in Kentucky, **United States of America** on 12 February, 1809.
He was a great **leader** and **humanist**.
He was one of the greatest presidents of the United States of America.

Abraham Lincoln loved reading. He felt that reading was important.

He read every book he could lay his hands on.

He also borrowed books from his neighbours.

Once, he walked 20 miles just to get a book.

Abraham Lincoln was very strong and healthy. He was very tall. In fact, he has been the tallest of all presidents of the United States of America.

Lincoln was a very honest and compassionate person. He was always ready to help people. People called him Honest Abe.

Once, Lincoln worked as a manager at a grocery store. One day, he happened to take a few extra **cents** from a customer by mistake. Lincoln discovered this at the end of the day.
He walked several miles to return the money to the customer.

Abraham Lincoln joined politics in 1832, at the young age of 23.
Yet, he won an election to the **Illinois** State Legislature in 1834.
He served the state government of Illinois for four successive terms.

Lincoln always wanted to become a lawyer.
He taught himself law by reading books.

In 1837, Abraham Lincoln became a lawyer.
He practiced law in Springfield, Illinois.
He also travelled throughout Illinois to work on cases as a lawyer. He soon became a successful lawyer.
Lincoln served eight years in the Illinois **legislature**.

Abraham Lincoln won the presidential **elections** of 1860.
He was elected as the sixteenth President of the United
States of America.
He took the oath of office on 4 March, 1861 in
Washington, D.C.

Lincoln was elected as President again in 1864.

During Abraham Lincoln's time, many people in the United States of America owned **slaves**. Lincoln believed that the United States of America stood for freedom for all.

He did not believe in slavery and worked hard to abolish it.

At that time, many states in the southern part of the United States of America did not agree with Abraham Lincoln. They declared that they were not a part of the United States of America.

This event led to the **American Civil War**. It began in April 1861.

Lincoln's **Union** Army fought the **Confederate** Army. Many soldiers were hurt and killed during the war. Finally, Lincoln's Union Army won the Civil War.

Abraham Lincoln loved reading, thinking and learning throughout his life. He showed great courage during the American Civil War. We can learn many things from him.

Lincoln was assassinated in Washington D.C., USA on 15 April, 1865.

Timeline

1837
Becomes a lawyer

1800   1810   1820   1830

1809
Born in the United
States of America

Abraham Lincoln's Life and Work

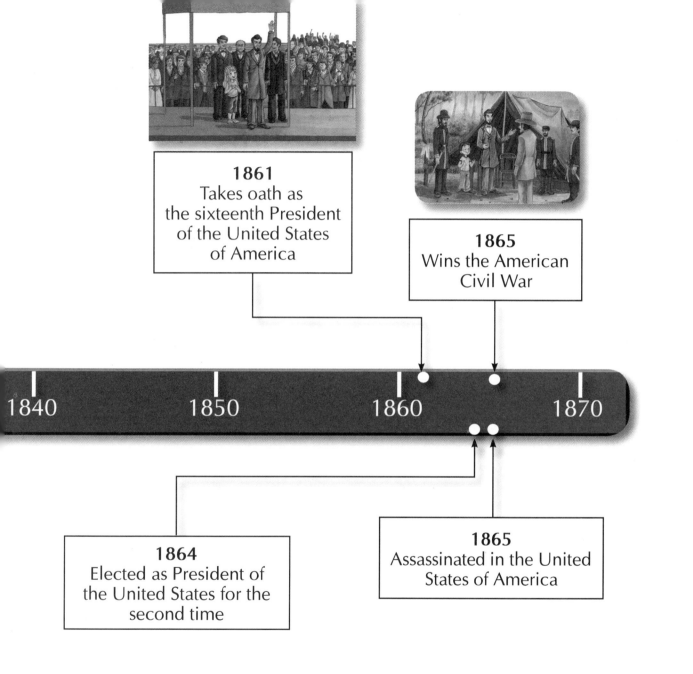

1861
Takes oath as
the sixteenth President
of the United States
of America

1865
Wins the American
Civil War

1840   1850   1860   1870

1864
Elected as President of
the United States for the
second time

1865
Assassinated in the United
States of America

Word Meanings

American Civil War: A major war in the United States of America between the government and the southern states

Assassinated: To murder a famous or important person, especially for political reasons

Confederate: A name used to refer to the 13 southern states that broke away from the United States of America

Cent: Currency in the United States of America. 100 cents is one US dollar

Election: Voting and choosing a candidate to govern the country

House of Representatives: A group of people who make the laws

Humanist: A person who believes that humans have the right to shape their own lives

Illinois: A state in the north central part of the United States of America

Leader: A person who guides others

Legislature: A group of elected people who create and change the laws

Slave: A person who is owned by someone

Union: Another name for the United States of America during the Civil War

United States: A large country in North America

Washington, D.C.: The capital city of United States of America

Think, Talk and Write

Think About It

Read the chapter again. Why do you think Abraham Lincoln was a great leader?
Think about his qualities.
Can you think of some other great leaders?

Talk About It

Tell your family or friends about Lincoln.
Tell them why you think slavery was bad.
Ask what they know about Lincoln.
Explain the other events of his life.

Write About It

Lincoln fought to bring slavery to an end. Did he succeed in his aim?
What would you like to do for your country? Write three lines telling
what would you do and why.

What did you learn from Abraham Lincoln?

....

....

....

....

....

....

....

....

....

....

....

....

....

What are the five things that you will change after reading Abraham Lincoln's story?

....

....

....

....

....

....

....

....

....

....

....

....

....

....

Work Space